SHAME

SHAME

RUSS RAINEY

RAPHA PUBLISHING/WORD, INC.
HOUSTON AND DALLAS, TX

Shame
by Russ Rainey
Copyright © 1991. Rapha Publishing/
Word, Inc., Houston and Dallas, TX.

Scripture quotations are from the New
American Standard Bible © The Lockman
Foundation, 1960, 1962, 1963, 1968, 1971,
1972, 1973, 1975, 1977.

First Printing, 1991
ISBN: 0-945276-37-0
Printed in the United States of America

CONTENTS

THE FLIP SIDES OF SHAME

Shame may be the deepest and potentially the most destructive human emotion. From a psychotherapist's perspective, it also may be the most misunderstood and most unrecognized feeling people experience. Shame wears many disguises; it does not always look the way we expect it to look. Like opposite sides of a coin, it might appear dull, dingy, beat-up, and worthless—or bright, shiny, exquisitely detailed, and of great value.

For instance, a person who lives the addicted lifestyle of a street alcoholic could certainly be said to be affected by shame, but so is the workaholic church staff member who only feels good when he or she is helping others. Shame may be obvious in the background of a shy, isolated, and vulnerable young female who seems fearful of exposure. But the same shame also may be present, although less obvious, in her same-age friend who appears grandiose, self-centered, and confident. A loser in every comparison who feels constantly guilty and condemned may have no more shame than a controlling, blaming, manipulative person.

Night and Day

Such stark contrasts are obvious in the lives of Julie and Jeff, twins separated before age 1 when they were adopted by two separate families. Both children went to homes deemed appropriate by the adoption agency. Both families attended church regularly. But there the similarities ended.

Julie's adoptive father sexually abused her from the age of 3 to 11. Her mother, a sexual-abuse victim who had never revealed her secret to anyone, was a very passive, ineffective parent. Julie's older sister, the couple's biological child, had also been abused; she became a very anxious, compliant person. Julie, however, was the rebellious type. She became sexually active at an early age, abused a variety of drugs, and had many school problems. She was raped at age 20 by her boss in the parking lot of a nightclub.

As an adult, Julie married and quickly divorced her first abusive, alcoholic husband, only to discover that she was pregnant. She saw no alternative but to have an abortion. She later found a man who seemed very kind and caring but who was out of work. She had a secure job, so they got married. However, because of his own childhood trauma, he also needed a crutch and was revealed to be alcoholic. When he drank, he was almost as cruel as Julie's first husband had been. They had children, and Julie sank into a life of trying to make the marriage work and the kids happy.

Making everyone happy and keeping her husband from throwing away everything for alcohol was not easy. To cope, Julie began to overeat, and over a five-year period she gained more than 100 pounds. By the time she sought help from her church, she was suicidal and almost totally unable to function in her family. The church referred her to a Christian counselor. As the counselor gently questioned her about her life, Julie sometimes wept uncontrollably. At other times she smiled inappropriately as she minimized the extent of her own abuse and her and her family's need for help. In her more honest moments, she admitted to being deeply depressed, having no self-worth, and feeling isolated from her acquaintances. She also had a fear of being left alone and at times had felt she was "going crazy." She described a desperate need for the love of a man, yet she was intensely afraid of men, especially those in authority. Her unshared memories of childhood sexual abuse and now-frequent nightmares were a new concern to her.

Jeff's history unfolded quite differently. Jeff's adoptive father was a well-respected businessman who owned his own business. He was a pillar of the church and community, but Jeff rarely saw him, much less spent time with him. His dad was either at work, at a church committee meeting, or playing golf. The time Jeff had with his father at home was not that enjoyable anyway, because his father was very strict and rigid with the two children (Jeff had a younger sister, also adopted). Jeff's mother had high expectations for her children. She was perfectionistic in her demands and managed to control almost everything Jeff and his sister thought, felt, ate, and wore.

As Jeff grew older, he became obsessed with achieving a high level of performance in school and sports. He also needed to be in the most popular crowd constantly to feel accepted. He had girlfriends, but most of his relationships were shallow and sexual. Jeff was charismatic but had no intimacy skills. He looked great throughout high school and college, yet no one knew that Jeff was masking depression and had begun to seek out secret sexual partners.

After he finished college, Jeff got a job with a large, nationally known corporation in which long hours and total commitment were the pathways to success. He married a young woman he had known for years in his church youth group, and they had two beautiful children. However, by age 30 Jeff had developed ulcers; one year later, his wife found out about his recent affairs with several other women.

He was not willing to go to counseling until his wife threatened him with the loss of his children. Then he complied and went to a Christian counselor "for her." The counselor observed that Jeff appeared haughty, self-assured, and in control. He denied having any problems, himself, but he angrily blamed his wife for not knowing how to love him and for nagging him about being gone from home so much. As the rapport deepened between Jeff and the nonjudgmental counselor, it became obvious that Jeff had an intense fear of failure. He could not handle criticism, and despite his outward image, he was confused, lonely, and depressed. In addition to the addictions of workaholism and perfectionism that Jeff had inherited from his parents, he also had become sexually addicted. He admitted that he felt near the edge of destruction with those behaviors.

Julie and Jeff's stories are as different as night and day, but the same shame operates in both of their lives. It is easy to note the shame of Julie's sexual abuse, but can you also see the shame in Jeff's self-worth being based on his achievements? It is obvious that

Julie acted in some noticeably shameful ways as a teenager, but Jeff carries equal shame for his secret sexual behavior. And although it's easy to look at Julie as an adult and say "what a pity, what a shame," it's less obvious—but just as certain—that Jeff's plastic lifestyle and compulsive behavior will ultimately bring him to ruin.

Both Julie and Jeff are eaten up with shame and guilt. They need an understanding of what shame is, where it comes from, and how it differs from true guilt.

Understanding Shame and Guilt

Theologians and psychologists alike have written extensively about guilt for many decades. Shame, however, has not received much attention until the last few years. The media have now made it difficult, if not impossible, to ignore the darker side of humanity. Everything seems to be "out of the closet," including addictions of every kind, physical and sexual abuse, and abortion. It's doubtful that the shame and guilt of such actions will ever again be entirely relegated to the secrecy of the closet.

What is shame, what is guilt, and how do they differ? A primary difference is that shame has to do with one's *being* while guilt has to do with one's *behavior*. Let's first look at shame's connection with the *being* aspect. Shame involves two basic components. The first component is the *exposure* of who we are, of that which is personal, private, or protected. For example, we do not want our bodies, our personal limitations, or our needs for worth, love, security, belonging, and dependency exposed inadvertently. This has to do with our identity. When we are exposed for who we really are and what we really need, we are then set up for the second component of shame: the *evaluation* of our being by the person to whom we have been exposed.

We fear others' evaluation or judgment because we sense that if we are found lacking we will be devalued, or even abandoned. Thus, shame occurs when we are exposed for who we really are, and as a result, we experience devaluation. This leads to a feeling of worthlessness. Shame, however, may also be induced by merely anticipating or recalling an experience of exposure and devaluation.

My own background serves as an illustration of this phenomenon. Growing up in a small, West Texas town where "men are men and sissies are not," I learned early on that crying is absolutely forbidden for a "real man." Although I know better now and have learned the benefit of tears and the honest expression of emotions, I still feel very vulnerable and exposed when tears seem to be welling up in my eyes. Then I feel not only the sadness that is causing the tears, but also shame in anticipation of exposing who I really am. I worry that if I cut loose and show myself for the sometimes-sensitive person I am, then someone else will consider me weak. And as a result, I will devalue myself.

Before we go further, though, let's make a distinction between *shame* and *fallenness*. Because we are fallen, sinful beings, we have limitations. Our acceptance of these limitations promotes the development of humility and self-acceptance. We admit that we are not omniscient or omnipotent. Acceptance of ourselves and our limitations is an admission that we are not God. We are not unlimited. We are just human and fallible. We also realize that we are not sufficient by ourselves.

We need others, but that does not diminish our worth. It leads us to search for someone greater than we are, someone we can go to for help. It leads us to God, Who values us. So if we accept our limitations and know that God values us, then exposure makes us aware of what we really need. And it is at that point when God intervenes in our lives.

In contrast, Genesis chapters 1 and 2 describe how Adam and Eve moved from acceptance of themselves and their God-given limitations to destructive shame. Adam and Eve were created in God's image and were given great authority over the earth, but nevertheless they had obvious limitations in comparison with the Creator. Realizing those limitations was healthy for them. The Bible says they were naked (which may also symbolize that they were open, honest, and had nothing to hide) and unashamed. That is, they were naked and unashamed until they were deceived and then became dissatisfied with their humanity and their limitations (i.e., their lack of knowledge of good and evil, which was reserved for God only). They wanted to become something more than what they were by eating the forbidden fruit of the tree of the knowledge of good and evil. Then, upon realizing their exposure, they devalued themselves in anticipation of God's devaluing their worth. They hid in shame, rejecting themselves and God's love and forgiveness.

The destructive effects of shame occur when we do not accept our own limitations or needs and they become exposed. Then we judge ourselves—or others find us— less valuable because of those limitations. We see ourselves as being much too vulnerable and open to judgment. Others often judge us negatively or take advantage of us because of this vulnerability. Then we feel certain that we are worthless and abandoned. Our thinking goes something like this: *If someone I love and trust devalues me (i.e., criticizes, takes advantage of, or uses me), then who can be trusted to reflect my value? If this person finds no value in me, there must be none. Therefore, I am valueless, worthless, fatally flawed, a big mistake—nothing!* We have been examined and found wanting.

Think of a young child who is being physically abused by a parent. Shame begins because of the child's inability to accept or even conceive of his or her childhood limitations: being too young, too powerless, or too fearful to protect himself or herself, or to tell someone who can. Because those facts are exposed and then taken advantage of, the child is left with no way to conceptualize what is happening except to believe that he or she is worthless.

Now let's look at how shame differs from guilt. While shame deals with our being or our worth, guilt pertains to our doing or our behavior. Guilt indicates *I failed*, while shame says *I am a failure*. Guilt is the feeling of condemnation for having made a mistake or having committed a sin. For Christians, however, Christ's forgiveness paid for our sins and condemnation. Now, for believers, the Holy Spirit's role is to convict—not condemn—us when we sin. His goal is restoration, not punishment.

Some authors describe the role of man's conscience as "constructive guilt." This type of guilt, they assert, is necessary to keep our behavior within certain boundaries and make us trustworthy members of society. As the source of constructive guilt, the conscience shapes our values, limits, and boundaries which are developed during childhood. A child who lives within firm but loving and consistent limits in a trustworthy cnvironment knows he or she is fallible yet worthwhile. In this environment, the child develops self-acceptance, trust, and a healthy conscience. Also in this setting, guilt leads to conviction, not to condemnation, and to repentance and restitution, not to regret. The conscience provides checks and balances which bring us back into our relationships with God and others.

When feelings of guilt emit from a person's shame-based worthlessness and self-hatred, that guilt is powerfully destructive. All guilt involves fear of punishment, but persons whose guilt evolves from shame believe they are so disgusting that they could never be punished enough for their deeds. So they never allow themselves to get "off the hook." In contrast, people who feel the Spirit's conviction of their sins know that confession and restitution can bring forgiveness. For those who feel ashamed, guilty, and worthless, there seems to be no amount of penance that can cancel the debt. Shame and guilt get enmeshed in an escalating cycle of shame, fear of abandonment, anger over the abandonment, guilt over the anger felt toward the person, then more shame, more guilt, and the downward spiral continues.

THE EFFECTS OF CHILDHOOD SHAMING ON ADULTS

The following discussion should be helpful in clarifying how someone who experienced shame in childhood might think, feel, and behave as an adult. This is not meant to be an exhaustive list of possible effects, but it may be useful in discovering whether or not shame has had a deciding impact on one's life. Because shame influences every area of a person's life, the effects are separated into the three components of personality: feeling, thinking, and behaving.

Feelings

Those who experienced shame in childhood may find themselves:

1. Feeling cut off from emotions (due to a lifetime of repressing them)
2. Feeling controlled by emotions that are painful and overwhelming
3. Feeling deeply wounded by abuse, abandonment, or addiction
4. Feeling anger or rage toward an offending person
5. Feeling depressed or constantly moody
6. Feeling anxiety and fear of:
   a. Exposure and vulnerability (due to lack of healthy boundaries)
   b. Intimacy
   c. Failure
   d. Rejection and abandonment
   e. Being violated or controlled by others
7. Feeling self-hatred, selfless, and shameful
8. Feeling grandiose and self-centered
9. Feeling ugly and incompetent
10. Feeling tremendous pride in appearance and superior to others
11. Feeling hopeless and helpless (often to the point of being suicidal)
12. Feeling intensely driven about self and life
13. Feeling overwhelmed, chaotic, and "crazy"
14. Feeling a lack of identity and confusion

15. Feeling guilty and apologetic
16. Feeling lonely, disconnected, and aimless

Thinking

Those who experienced shame in childhood may find themselves:

1. Believing they are inferior and others are superior
2. Believing they must compensate for inferiority and low self-worth by perfect appearance, achievements, and approval
3. Believing that abuse or suffering is deserved
4. Believing others also deserve blame, suffering, or abuse
5. Believing they cannot change, should not help themselves, and will never make a difference to anyone
6. Believing it is their responsibility to help, change, or control others
7. Believing others cannot be trusted
8. Believing others are trying to control them and being hypersensitive to any control issue
9. Believing that things and they, themselves, should be perfect (according to lots of

unwritten rules about the way things "should be")

10. Believing it's OK to lie under certain conditions
11. Believing that addictions are controllable and necessary to block pain
12. Believing that constant introspection, comparison with others, and trying to read their minds is beneficial

Behavior

Those who experienced shame in childhood may find themselves:

1. Avoiding relationships out of fear of intimacy and being hurt
2. Rushing into relationships because of the overwhelming need for acceptance
3. Going through numerous failed relationships
4. Staying with one long, miserable relationship
5. Tap dancing in a relationship (e.g., substituting sex for intimacy) instead of committing to the risk of intimacy

6. Fixing, rescuing, and controlling others
7. Blaming others to avoid feeling worse about oneself
8. Giving until it hurts (themselves and others)
9. Ignoring their own needs (because that would be selfish)
10. Focusing on bodily ills to the point of becoming a hypochondriac, or, conversely, ignoring dangerous physical symptoms
11. Expending enormous emotional and physical energy pleasing others, being religious, and being self-righteous
12. Bending the truth if necessary but at times revealing too much personal truth when not appropriate
13. Engaging in addictive, risky, or promiscuous behavior
14. Being the life of the party or having no spontaneity at all
15. Being passive, passive-aggressive, or aggressive—but not appropriately assertive
16. Engaging in a variety of overdoing behaviors to relieve the constant stress (i.e., overeating, oversleeping, overmedicating, overexercising, overcleaning, etc.)

IDENTIFYING SHAME-BASED FAMILY MODELS

As if it were not enough that, as fallen creatures, we all tend to devaluate ourselves, there are others who are often quite willing to devaluate or shame us for their own self-centered reasons. Families are great at this. Guilt and shame are universal parenting techniques used by mothers and fathers, both young and old.

Before we define why families and others shame children, let's understand one important point. The following paragraphs should not be construed as parent-bashing. Every parent does the best he or she can do based on experience, knowledge, skills, and emotional energy. We all get angry at a parent who physically or sexually abuses a child, but the truth is, in one form or another, we have all abused our children. Jesus' advice in Matthew 7:2 should ring in our ears: "For in the way you judge, you will be judged."

Parents who shame their children have never been able to escape the quicksand of shame, themselves. And because the source of shame is often well hidden, neither they nor their children may know the source of the problems. Most families have their secrets, but some are deeper and darker and more sickening than others. The secrets may have been kept over generations, but their power to make families sick in the present is incredible. Examples of such secrets include incest, mental illness, public humiliation, financial disaster, addiction, abandonment, and violence to self or others.

Parents shame their children because they cannot escape their own personal, ongoing, shameful, self-centered experiences. Many of them are living in very dysfunctional, conflict-filled marriages that provide no intimacy. They may be slaves to addictions, compulsions, or the drive to "fix" and control others. They may live under the constant stress of poor self-image and external control. They lack parenting skills and often lack the desire to parent. They are often purposeless, having no spirituality to help them overcome feelings of being trapped by work, marriage, and other circumstances.

Abandonment and Shame

Space does not allow a full explanation of the many ways families pass on their shame, but a broad explanation is that shame comes chiefly from abandonment. (Abuse will be seen later as a related category; in the eyes of the victim, abuse is also essentially abandonment.) Parents who have not dealt with their own shame issues do not have the emotional energy or resources to "be there" for their children. As much as they would love to, they don't know how. Their parenting difficulties often begin with failure in two of the most crucial of all child developmental issues: bonding and separating.

In the book *Your Parents and You*, Robert McGee explains that severe damage can occur to a child early in life—before age 2—if bonding does not occur.[1] Bonding is the emotional attachment of the child to the parent due to the parent's investment of love, physical contact, and time. The child's development of love, value, and identity depend on this bonding. It may not occur if the parents are incapacitated due to physical illness, mental illness, addiction, absence, death, or if they had no model, themselves. When parents are emotionally unavailable, distant, and unaffectionate, the child's self-perception is that something is wrong with him or her that keeps the parents from meeting the child's needs.

McGee also notes that blocked separation, another developmental process, may also cause emotional damage. Separation has to do with healthy independence from parents and with setting one's own limits and boundaries. Parents who grew up with their own burden of shame and had trouble with separation may go to one of two extremes here. They either avoid separation and smother the child with advice and correction, or they force separation and neglect the child.

Smothering says to the child, *You're not competent.* Neglect says, *You're not worth my time and effort.* Either way, abandonment seems real and shame results.

In its purest form, abandonment is the physical absence of a parent. Perfectionist parents who have learned to cover their own shame by seeking high levels of performance and approval express implied abandonment to their children. What comes across is, *Outside standards and others' approval are more important than you,* and *You either do it my way or else . . . .*

On some level, all of us know how abandonment feels. However, those who have been abandoned by a caregiver know it in a much more intense way. They grieve the loss, not of someone who was taken away, but of someone who seemingly walked away of his or her own accord. They feel empty, purposeless, hopeless, lonely, and worthy of no one's love. Some have described it as a "hole in the soul." That is not an acceptable, tolerable way to live. That person soon begins looking for something available and dependable to fill the hole. It could be drugs, sex, relationships, money, food, or whatever, as long as it "fills the hole."

Abandonment also sets one up for expecting a lifetime of more abandonment, and it usually materializes due to the types of people the abandoned person chooses for partners. For example, someone who was abandoned by his or her father will usually choose as a partner someone who possesses the father's traits. This is an unconscious effort to "fix" the original relationship and get what was missing. Tragically, the person who possesses the undependable father's traits is not very likely to be dependable! Abandonment strikes again.

The bottom-line conclusion of the person who experiences abandonment is, *It must be my fault. I must have done something terribly wrong. Maybe if I had been a better son or wife (or whatever) this wouldn't have happened. I must not deserve someone who will meet my needs. I don't deserve anything!*

Abuse and Shame

Abuse of any kind indicates to a child that he or she is an object of contempt, of no value except maybe to meet the abuser's needs. Strange as it may seem, though, abused kids often see their experience as normal, no matter how awful it is. They see their abusive parents as the source of love and value. That is how abuse totally skews children's perceptions of themselves, love, relationships, and God. No wonder they have a hard time relating to God later in life!

When we think of abuse, we normally think of physical abuse. It comes in several forms and intensities, ranging from a spanking to satisfy the anger of a normally kind parent to atrocious cult-ritual abuse in which unimaginable horrors are committed. Many abuses are performed under the influence of an addictive substance.

Abuse may also be verbal and emotional. Verbal abuse may include yelling, name-calling, humiliation, comparison, and criticism aimed at the child rather than at his or her behavior. Emotional abuse includes lying to a child, ignoring him or her, discounting the child's emotions and needs, having excessive expectations, disgust, or blaming the child for things he or she is not responsible for.

"Emotional incest" occurs, for example, when a male child is promoted to adult responsibilities to meet his mother's adult needs for intimacy and companionship because the father is physically or emotionally unavailable. These types of abuse are equally as damaging as physical abuse.

The most damaging of all abuse is probably sexual abuse. We will be astounded and sickened over the next decade as we get more accurate information on how often this tragedy actually happens. Already, informed estimates are that one out of every 10 families is experiencing incestuous abuse, and for every case reported, 25 cases remain unreported.[2] Sexual abuse occurs whenever someone uses a child for his or her own stimulation. It runs the gamut from abuse of the privacy boundary in the home to inappropriate comments, exposure to pornography, and certainly to any kind of touching for the abuser's stimulation. It says to a child, *You are useful to me as a sexual object but worthless as a person.* Unfortunately, the primary bait used to lure most victims into the experience is an offer of emotional intimacy, which in shameful families is precisely what children crave the most.

What effects do all of these shaming experiences have on children? Shame builds and feeds on itself, and as one layer of shame stacks on the others, the situation becomes progressively more difficult to admit to—much less stop. Abused children learn a model for perceiving and relating that is based on shame. They also borrow shame from parents who appear pitiful and helpless. Then all their future relationships are damaged as they act out what they know. Their view of God is greatly distorted. Their self-image and personal identity are nonexistent. They may become suicidal, abusive to themselves or to others, victimized, addicted, and unable to function due to feelings of anger, guilt, fear, loneliness, anxiety, and depression. They live their lives in chaos as the cycle of shame continues.

COPING WITH SHAME

Defense Mechanisms

How do shamed people cope? They find ingenious survival techniques to protect themselves. One category of protective techniques is called ego-defense mechanisms. They help people cope with unpleasant thoughts, memories, and feelings. All of us use these techniques from time to time, but it is very unhealthy to use them as a routine or rigid way of dealing with shame and anxiety. Examples of some common ego-defense mechanisms are denial (in which facts or events are excluded from reality), repression of feelings, perceptions, and memories (by pushing them into the unconscious), and dissociation (a psychological and/or emotional disengagement from reality in which the person imagines himself or herself as being somewhere else).

Recently, I went to a professional seminar on sexual abuse. I was there to earn professional continuing-education credit hours. But, as the speaker presented information about the variety of experiences that are abusive, I became aware that some of my childhood experiences with other children in my neighborhood had actually been abusive sexual experiences. At the time, I suppose we considered it as "initiation." The realization that it was actually abusive brought on a flood of repressed memories and feelings that I had to process later with others. It was a great relief to deal with those issues, but it was also strange to realize just how effective my repression had been.

Although defense mechanisms are automatic and unconscious, maintaining them requires great amounts of emotional energy. They do block out shame, but at what cost? Emotions that are not experienced cannot be healed. Therefore, these defense mechanisms cannot be called upon to deal with shame over a long period of time or else the mechanisms, themselves, become a problem.

Achievement and People-Pleasing

One of the most useful concepts for understanding how a person copes with shame is described by Robert McGee in his book, *The Search for Significance.* He explains that a person with low self-worth easily gets deceived by Satan into believing, *If I can only perform better and get certain significant people's approval, I will feel worthy.* Satan convinces people filled with shame that they will never be worthy as they are. They must do something to earn worth.[3]

Thinking through our achievement and people-pleasing behaviors is a good way for all of us to get in touch with the silent impact shame has on our lives. For example, people might say that I am a hard worker committed to my tasks, but if I were honest I would have to admit that I am a perfectionist and my self-worth cannot withstand criticism or failure on the job. Others might perceive me as a nice and considerate person, willing to go the extra mile, when the truth is that I have learned that the way to feel good about myself is to keep my approval rating up by being a nice guy. Admitting such truths is painful for most of us, because it exposes us for who we really are and clearly indicates that our motivation is shame.

We all do a certain amount of performing and people-pleasing to get positive responses. However, shamed people live and die by their ability to control their performance and others' opinions of them. These people fall into two basic categories, says McGee: those who become compulsively driven to control every situation, or those who withdraw and avoid taking any risk where failure is possible. These categories are not mutually exclusive, so one person may have a combination of both styles of coping.[4]

The problem with depending on our achievements and our ability to please others is that our best efforts are never enough to consistently maintain a feeling of adequate worth. Keeping self-worth "filled up" in this manner is like trying to keep a bucket with a hole in it filled with water.

Roles

People play a variety of roles throughout their lives. For instance, a person who compulsively strives to control performance and approval, as mentioned earlier, might become the family hero, the school's star athlete, and later in life, the boss's favorite. Although this particular role might seem advantageous, it is actually a soul killer because the person's real self never gains an identity or permanent worth. So worthlessness always seems to be just one failure away. Shame is perpetuated by the fear of failure or rejection—and certainly when failure actually occurs.

Another person might give up on pleasing and performing and react in anger and hostility, playing the role of the rebel. Seeing life as being all too serious and intense, others may adopt the role of a clown, making a joke out of everything and being irrelevant and irreverent. Yet another person may see no roles that he or she could fill and become simply a wallflower, watching the world go by and wishing for a place to jump on it. Then there are the Florence Nightingales, people who take on the world and all its problems; they try to fix everything and anyone.

As with any coping mechanism, though, the rigid overuse of a role causes it to become restrictive and stale. The role begins to define the person rather than the other way around. And eventually, it doesn't work at all. Everyone knows that rebels lose their charm as they grow older. A happy face on a clown doesn't make for peace and joy on the inside. Wallflowers fade away very quickly if they don't get some nurturing and sunshine, and Florence Nightingales usually burn out while burning the candle at both ends.

Thus, in answer to the question, "How do shamed people cope?" we must say they do the best they can, but it's never enough. Then the failure of their coping techniques brings more shame. That's when they begin to look for something else to help them relieve or escape the pain. And that is when addictions and compulsive behavior enter the scene.

Addictions

Addictions are also unhealthy techniques for dealing with shame. What they offer the victim of shame is the myth of control. Being able to control feeling good, if even for a short while, seems well worth the consequences. Then if a rare good moment does occur (such as when one's performance is pleasing or when approval is attained), what better way to celebrate than to enhance the high with another high? Once the myth of control is well entrenched as a coping mechanism, addiction can be used to alter the whole spectrum of human emotions from depression, anger, hopelessness, or boredom—to ecstatic pleasure.

Addiction comes in many forms, and it is not limited to external substances such as alcohol, drugs, or food. People can also be addicted to external experiences such as gambling, shopping, religiosity, sexual experience, perfectionism, and relationships. One can be addicted to an internal substance, too, such as one's own adrenaline (thrill seeking) or to internal experiences such as fantasy, worry, or rage. All these addictions offer the same myth: *I can control myself, others, and events, and therefore I can meet my own needs.*

Our families often have much to do with which addictions we employ. Parents model their own addictions for their children. This is easy to see with the alcoholic, yet just as true for the person addicted to rage. In fact, families may unwittingly offer their children all three avenues that can lead to addiction: (1) genetic predisposition, which makes children of alcoholic parents and grandparents much more likely or predisposed to become alcoholics if they choose to drink, (2) prolonged, repetitive exposure to an addictive substance or experience leading to tolerance and addiction (i.e., a baby given alcohol or sedatives in its bottle to "keep it calmed down" will likely have a drug problem later, and a child who lives with a father's addictive rage may learn to tolerate it and may become a rageaholic, too), and (3) high stress produced by both the chaos of a dysfunctional, addictive family and the internal stress of low self-worth.

Addiction extracts a high price from its deluded victim. Ironically, the myth of complete control evolves into a life that is out of control and unbalanced in every way. Thinking becomes distorted and irrational.

Emotions are repressed and waiting to explode. Relationships are deeply damaged, if not destroyed. Consequences are severe (loss of job, health, family, finances), and any remaining self-worth is destroyed. Another coping mechanism bites the dust.

If those who are addicted are involved in such self-destruction, why don't they just stop? They can't. In Romans 7:21–23 the apostle Paul admitted that he, too, was plagued with such a dilemma:

> I find then the principle that evil is present in me, the one who wishes to do good. For I joyfully concur with the law of God in the inner man, but I see a different law in the members of my body, waging war against the law of my mind, and making me a prisoner of the law of sin which is in my members.

Addiction is a trap that willpower cannot overcome. It is an effort to deal with shame; but the addiction, itself, becomes a source of shame. The consequences of addiction deepen the shame, and although the addiction eventually loses its power to give the desired effect, it has already become the person's lover, his or her god—everything. It cannot be given up without extreme difficulty and lots of help. Addictions, like other techniques for self-protection, are useless to defeat the power of shame in our lives.

SHAME'S EFFECT ON CURRENT RELATIONSHIPS

Those who carry shame and have little or no self-worth may settle for a life of seclusion, but most often they seek out relationships with others whom they hope can provide what is lacking in their lives. Their belief is, *If I can find someone who will love me, I will have been proven to be lovable. Then I will love myself, I will be able to love, and we will be happy forever*. Don't we all wish that were reality?

Human nature is strange. In our fallen delusion we have come up with a foolproof formula for getting what we need from an intimate relationship. First we look around for someone who feels familiar, someone who has traits similar to our opposite-sex parent. Then we begin relating to him or her in the same old dysfunctional ways we related to our parents at home. By doing that we believe we will get the other person to meet our needs that were not met at home while we were growing up. That hardly sounds like the formula for a successful relationship, does it?

But we do look for the familiar, because that is what we understand and relate to the best. For instance, if we had an enmeshed, overdependent relationship with a parent, then we may look for someone else to take care of us. If, on the other hand, our parents were needy people who needed taking care of, themselves, or who left us to take care of other siblings as a parent would, then we may look for someone to care for, rescue, and fix.

When we find that special someone, we set about getting from them what we lacked at home—unconditional love and nurturance. We may have gotten none at home, or maybe we got some but it didn't come in a form we could accept. At any rate, we understand that this person we are marrying is supposed to meet all of our unmet needs for love, security, acceptance, and worth.

When those expectations don't work out exactly as we had planned, disappointment sets in and we fall back into getting our needs met the way we did in our family of origin. Several different tacks can be used to force the spouse to give what's needed. A person might become demanding, controlling, manipulative, or even rageful to force the spouse into acting. Or a person might try the super-sweet approach, fawning all over the other and even being seductive. If that doesn't work, there is always the "poor-me" routine with lots of self-pity and maybe even real depression. Those who grew up with too much responsibility too early in life seem to prefer the martyr approach, exhibiting over-responsibility so the spouse feels guilty and indebted. And one other very effective ploy is to become isolated from the spouse, making him or her feel even more abandoned than the disappointed partner.

Couples do get blinded by the myth of wedded bliss. Before marriage, we see our prospective spouse as trustworthy and capable of providing everything we need, only to find out rather quickly that such is not the case. When trust is sufficiently broken, it brings back all of the old repressed feelings and memories of shattered trust that existed in the family of origin. The spouse who has "failed" then gets the distrust that was actually "earned" by all the partner's past offenders. This soon becomes a pattern: As distrust is expressed, the spouse reacts in anger; that anger is perceived by the partner as rejection, and the rejection proves that the offending spouse was, indeed, not trustworthy.

The point is, when the reality of life sets in, shame and blame begin. Each person in this kind of dysfunctional relationship is dealing with his or her own disappointment. But, blind to their own individual processes, both of them see the relationship or the other person as the problem.

For example, when a married couple argues, the point of interaction for both spouses is focused on a present relationship issue such as "You always ignore me at the breakfast table," or "All you want to do is talk all the time." What seems obvious to each spouse is that the relationship is not working and, plainly, the other person is at fault.

Not so obvious are all the shame-based beliefs, abusive experiences, and protective mechanisms that are driving the current state of affairs. There is no chance of having healthy, here-and-now, intimate communication when both partners are caught up in their own unresolved issues of shame.

Each such interaction that passes unresolved adds yet another brick to the wall of hostility, anger, and resentment. Each separate incident carries its own burden of guilt and shame. Added together, these "little" burdens deliver another giant blow against each individual's sense of worth. Each spouse has failed at life's most important human relationship, marriage. And shame marches on.

Now let's take a moment to review. To this point, we have looked at shame and devaluation of self. We have seen that shame is perpetuated by various forms of abuse. We have noted how each of us seeks to protect himself or herself from shame and how the failure of that protection creates more layers of shame. Finally, we see that the illusion of being saved from shame by loving human relationships is a mirage.

By now you may be feeling like Paul did when he wrote, "Wretched man that I am! Who will set me free from the body of this death?" (Romans 7:24). But there is hope for us today, just as there was for Paul. In the next verse he proclaims the answer: "Jesus Christ our Lord!"

Let's now turn our attention to a process of recovery that uses this answer, glorifying God and resolving our shame.

RESOLVING SHAME

A miserable, self-centered little boy in C. S. Lewis's book, *The Voyage of the "Dawn Treader,"* (New York: Collier Books, 1978) went to sleep in a dragon's cave and woke up appearing outwardly what he already was inwardly—a dragon. Like this unhappy boy, some of us have grown increasingly aware that we are dragons. We may be hurting intensely on the inside, but what others see on the outside is an armor of thick, thorny scales of protection and a propensity to breathe fire when stormy emotions are awakened within us. Dragons in mythology were often people under a curse, and in this situation, so are we.

I dislike thinking about myself as a fire-breathing dragon, and when I'm not occupied with hiding my true reality, I have, from time to time, made decent efforts toward changing. I am sad to say, though, that all of my best efforts have merely scratched at protective scales, only to find another layer of scales underneath. Only when I have risked allowing Jesus and others to see me for what I really am, and have accepted their unconditional love for me have I been able to let go and let God transform my life. His methods and timing have rarely been acceptable to me in the short term, but they have certainly proven faithful, healing, and life-giving as I have accepted them. The information that follows on resolving shame is written from both a clinical perspective and my own experience.

The Essentials

Resolving shame involves accepting two basic realities and working through four necessary actions. The realities must be accepted and maintained throughout the recovery process or relapse will occur. The first reality is, *I am not in control and cannot meet my own needs*. The second reality is, *God is in control, and He is the only One I can ultimately rely on*. The four actions are (1) revealing the true self, (2) redirecting, (3) replacing the old with the new, and (4) reestablishing intimacy.

The first reality or realization, *I am not in control and cannot meet my own needs*, only comes through pain. It means a person must break through the protective denial and admit that he or she needs help. Denial is broken for some only through severe suffering, injury, loss, exhaustion, and humiliation. Only after hitting such a "bottom" can some of us begin to earnestly look for sources of help. That help may include books, seminars, groups, or professional or qualified lay counselors. It certainly should include God. However, at this early stage many are still resentful of God and cannot accept His love and resources.

That brings us to reality number two: *God is in control, and He is the only One I can ultimately rely on*. In most cases this realization comes slowly; it is not accepted due to *hearing* sermons, but due to *seeing* sermons lived out by others who have been there ahead of us. It may take a long time to truly accept God and rely only on Him. But the longer we walk in our own light, the longer we will be in pain. Isaiah 50:7–11 tells us that even when we have to walk through the darkness we will not have to be ashamed or afraid—if we walk in God's light. However, if we light our own fire, encircle ourselves with our own light, and walk in that light, then we will "lie down in torment."

Now let's look at the four actions that help resolve shame.

Revealing the True Self

Honesty. If there is one thing that serves as a key to unlock the door into recovery, that is it. A person's healing journey can begin only after he or she allows honest exposure of who he or she really is. Remember, though, that this is where shame begins, with exposure of the self. It is ironic that without this same exposure no healing can come. One must risk exposure to regain a connection with others, to regain validation of oneself. Revealing the true self should be done with a trustworthy and confidential person or group such as a counselor or support group. It should not be rushed. Most of us have layers upon layers of defenses, repressed memories, and feelings covering up other memories and feelings. We should be patient with ourselves—as God is. He will reveal to us what we need to expose, one thing at a time.

Revelation of the self happens on several levels. Current relationships are usually the easiest place to begin looking for signs of shame. Living in shame means a person has learned to live in hatred of self, others, and God. Such hatred cannot be hidden. It shows itself through our marriage relationships, parenting, relationships with our own parents and family of origin, and through conflict-filled or superficial relationships with others all around us. It certainly shows itself in our lack of a deep and personal relationship with Jesus Christ. It shows through even our best efforts to mask it. And only when it is revealed can it be addressed.

Supporting such hatred are the self-destructive beliefs we mentioned earlier regarding performing for others and trying to win their approval. They, too, must be revealed. Admitting that performance and approval are gods we serve is a first step toward letting go of our resentment toward those who (we believe) demand performance and withhold approval of us.

Addictions and compulsions must also be revealed. They require denial to continue and are extremely humiliating to reveal, especially those that are hidden or have a heavy stigma attached. Exposing the ugliness of addiction and finding the listener accepting gives badly needed hope to the addicted person and begins relieving shame.

One of the most obvious tip-offs that a person is carrying a load of shame is the presence of one or more addictions in his or her life. Addiction is the smoke that follows the fire of shame. Dealing with shame means getting help first for the addiction, whether it is drug and alcohol abuse, eating disorders, codependency (the compulsion to fix, rescue, and control others), sexual addiction, or any others. These activities are so life-consuming that they must be adequately treated first as the primary disorder because they can be life-threatening. The same can be said for other types of major disorders such as depression, anxiety, and psychosis. All of these major disorders and addictions require treatment prior to and during the treatment for alleviating shame.

Few revelations are more difficult than telling about being victimized by someone who was trusted, especially by sexual abuse. Because of dissociation, the defense mechanism mentioned earlier, a victim may have difficulty even remembering specific events. However, as trust is built with the listener and as events are remembered, revealing them brings back blocked feelings that have been manifesting themselves in other destructive ways. These victims often ask, "Is it absolutely essential that I talk to someone about the actual details of the abuse?" The answer is "yes." Those repressed details hold deep emotions captive. If those emotions are not released, they will continue to seep out like toxic waste, destroying the quality of the victim's life. This type of revelation is best done with a listener who has significant expertise in dealing with such abuse, such as a professional counselor.

Another type of revelation involves the admission of and grieving for losses. The shame-based, dysfunctional family creates many of them, including loss of life, loss of health, loss of childhood, loss of relationships, loss of identity, and self-worth. The list could go on and on. Revealing losses requires a person to work through the grieving process with another person or face the possibility that the next loss (and life is full of them) could be "the straw that breaks the camel's back."

Revealing or exposing the real self is difficult, indeed. But when one risks exposure and the listener responds with love and acceptance, it brings back a desperately needed sense of belonging, worth, and connectedness to the world.

Redirecting

The word *redirecting* here means essentially the same thing as the biblical word *repentance*. In this discussion, *redirecting* means "turning away from something that dishonors God and is bad for us." Some of us have grown up understanding repentance as including self-degradation or condemnation.

That is not what is meant here. Legitimate sorrow over the direction of one's past actions does not necessitate self-condemnation. Repenting or redirecting oneself does not have to be a morbid, negative experience.

To the contrary, repenting implies a positive use of free will and choice, of the God-given power to change. Second Corinthians 7:9–13 speaks of this positive force of repentance. It does involve sorrow, but it is a sorrow leading to life, not death, to caring, not apathy, to acting, not just reacting, and to feeling a zeal for life instead of regret. In James 4:6–10, God tells us that if we are sorrowful over our sins, particularly of pride, *He* will lift us up.

Certainly redirecting means turning away from particular perceptions and attitudes. One particularly troublesome but understandable perception held by many persons who were abused and shamed as children is, *God was not there when I was being abused. Where was He?* It is critical that a person turn from this perception of God. Recovery from shame and abuse is a process of working through and expressing the feelings related to abandonment by others. One of those feelings is resentment. We resent others for their abuse and God for His passivity. It is important to realize, though, that God can handle our feelings. He would prefer that we express our negative feelings toward Him than continue in the belief that He doesn't care. The prophecy of Isaiah (chapter 53) predicted that Christ would bear all our griefs and sorrows on the cross. And He did. He experienced our abuse. He also died for our abusers' iniquities. He was there for us. We must learn to see Him as He is, both loving and just, always faithful.

We also must turn from any view we have of ourselves and others as being worthless, forsaken, hopeless beings—or in the common vernacular, "jerks," "idiots," "nerds," and "dorks." If we are children of God, God sees us as objects of His love (1 John 4:9–11), totally justified in His sight (Romans 5:1), holy, blameless, beyond reproach (Colossians 1:21–22), and absolutely complete in Christ (Colossians 2:10). For us to judge ourselves any other way is sin.

For us to judge others is also sin. As mentioned earlier, God warns us in Matthew 7:1–2 that we will be judged the same way we judge others. He reminds us in chapter 5 that He looks not only on our outward actions but also on our hearts.

Colossians 3 advises us to "put off" the deeds of the old nature. This means we should turn from our known sinful patterns, many of which are listed in that passage. But we could also include addictions and/or compulsions, dishonesty, self-defeating beliefs, resentment, and much more. If putting off or turning from our sinful patterns were something we could easily do by ourselves, though, we wouldn't be in the mess we are in now, would we? No, it's not easy and it cannot be done solely by ourselves. We need help. We need support and encouragement. We need new role models, affirmation, and a new course that clearly shows us a new, healthier direction.

A person can find all of the above under one roof at a 12-step recovery group. The same 12 steps that have helped millions recover from alcoholism are proving to be equally powerful in the lives of those weighed down by shame. The steps are simply biblical principles in layman's terms; they guide one through the scriptural processes of regeneration and sanctification. Oddly enough, most 12-step groups in the past have met apart from the church. Presently, though, many churches are realizing the necessity for and the benefit of such groups, and many have already begun them. For some people, turning from disabling behaviors and beliefs will require additional professional help, but everyone can take advantage of the help and hope of a Christ-centered support group.

Replacing the Old with the New

In Colossians 3:12–15, we are admonished that it is not enough to simply "turn from" our old ways. We must "turn to" or "put on" something new. Paul states,

> And so, as those who have been chosen of God, holy and beloved, put on a heart of compassion, kindness, humility, gentleness and patience; bearing with one another, and forgiving each other, whoever has a complaint against anyone; just as the Lord forgave you, so also should you. And beyond all these things put on love, which is the perfect bond of

unity. And let the peace of Christ rule
in your hearts, to which indeed you
were called in one body; and be
thankful.

The Bible calls this "renewing" our minds.

Romans 12:2 tells us that God has given
us this task of renewing our minds. It is a
lifelong process, a daily assignment, and a
moment-by-moment challenge. In *The Search
for Significance*, Robert S. McGee suggests
that renewing the mind includes focusing on
what *God* has done *for us* (i.e., justification,
reconciliation, propitiation, and regeneration)
and therefore, what is *true of us* (that we are
"deeply loved, completely forgiven, fully
pleasing, totally accepted, and complete in
Christ").[5]

Replacing the old with the new means
that we learn to trace our destructive emotions
back to their ungodly sources, our inaccurate
beliefs, and then reject those beliefs. Then
we can replace them with the truth found in
God's Word. Again, this process is not
necessarily simple or easy, but it is extremely
effective and gets easier with practice.

As an example of the process, let's say a man often gets anxious to the point of almost having a panic attack each time his boss summons him. If the man were to stop and think, he might realize that his anxious feelings probably come from the inaccurate belief that his worth is dependent on getting his boss's approval, and he is afraid of losing it. He could then reject that belief as inaccurate and destructive and choose to remember that, to God, he is totally acceptable (Colossians 1:21–22). He needs no one's approval but God's to have a feeling of worth. He will still want to apply himself on the job, but with some practice in confronting his belief, he can stop being anxious about his boss's approval.

Replacing the old with the new not only has to do with accepting and incorporating Christ's perception of us and His forgiveness, it also has to do with forgiving and loving others as Christ forgives and loves us. Shame is passed on through the generations primarily because forgiveness and love are not part of people's lives. God knows the truth about what is in our hearts and is more than firm with His stance on forgiveness. In Matthew 6:14–15, Christ says, "For if you forgive men for their transgressions, your heavenly Father will also forgive you. But if you do not forgive men, then your Father will not forgive your transgressions." Tough words. Can we afford to ignore them?

The issue of forgiveness is extremely sensitive for many who have encountered abuse from a loved one. Unfortunately, as Christians we often make forgiveness more difficult for damaged persons by unwisely recommending it too early in the healing process. Forgiveness should not be pushed on anyone, but it is necessary to completely resolve one's shame.

Forgiveness does not mean ignoring the damage done by the abuse, acting as if everything is all right, and then continuing to be a target for more abuse. In his book, *The Wounded Heart*, author Dan Allender bases his definition of love on Christ's command in Matthew 5:44 to love our enemies. He defines it as "the free gift that voluntarily cancels the debt in order to free the debtor to become what he might be if he experiences the joy of restoration." Forgiveness, then, says Allender, involves three things: "(1) a hunger for restoration, (2) bold love, and (3) revoked revenge."[6] A person who has deeply experienced the forgiveness of his or her own sin will eventually hunger for restoration.

Reestablishing Intimacy

We were created for intimacy by an intimate God. We crave intimacy when it is missing. It was in our family group that intimacy was lost, dishonesty and secret-keeping were learned, distrust developed, and the expression of emotion was disabled. It is in a substitute family, a support group, that intimacy can be relearned, secrets revealed, trust restored, and emotions expressed. Reestablishing intimacy with God often happens only after a person enters the intimate process of sharing openly with others and seeing their unconditional love. It is as if we must experience creature love before we can understand and accept the Creator's love.

The process of reestablishing intimacy is a difficult and tedious one indeed. It requires a great deal of risk. It means enduring the awkwardness of getting or giving a hug if you're not used to it. It means exposing parts of your inner-self that you have a hard time admitting even exist. It means facing the fear of rejection when you speak out about what is actually going on inside of you. It is not easy, but it is definitely worth the effort.

Reestablishing intimacy is best done in a supportive group that acts as a substitute family because there one can find acceptance by others who really do understand the pain. There one can be truly listened to, maybe for the first time, without being corrected or condemned by someone else. There one can find a sense of belonging that was never experienced in the family.

A person who has lived with shame has great difficulty experiencing the deep, personal familiarity and closeness that we call intimacy. Very often children are lured into abuse by the prospect of experiencing intimacy. This is certainly the case with much sexual abuse. Therefore, that which later promises intimacy (i.e., marriage or substitute family groups) is greatly feared. There is, however, no way to reestablish intimacy other than to take the necessary risks.

A person's first reaction to the idea of substitute family support groups is usually, "No thanks, I don't do well in groups." Well, of course not. Groups remind the person of his or her family, and that isn't a good memory. Nevertheless, supportive groups remain the single best tool for experimenting with and practicing intimacy. Talk to people who have attended groups for several months or years. They cannot always put into words *why* the groups help, but they will assure you that they do.

Who's in Control?

How many times have I seen it? Again and again, people enter a Rapha Hospital Treatment Center as though they have both hands on the steering wheel and one foot on the gas pedal and the other on the brake. They are doing their absolute best to keep life under their own control. However, as they begin integrating into the loving environment of the Christian staff and patients and see that this is a place where a person can reveal the true self, there comes the realization that *I am not in control. Believing that I was in control is what got me here!*

Honesty has begun; shame begins to crack. Eventually, old beliefs, feelings, and behaviors are revealed as ungodly and unhealthy. Life-changing decisions are made to redirect life into new, healthy channels. Tools are learned that enable replacement of old, destructive beliefs with new life-enhancing beliefs. And intimacy is experienced as secrets are revealed, trust is restored, and emotions are expressed in an accepting substitute family group. Shame melts away.

Only God can orchestrate such healing, and throughout the treatment process people come to realize that others may hurt them again, but God can always be relied upon for healing.

CONCLUSION

Recovery from the destructive effects of shame involves accepting Christ's promise that, "you shall know the truth, and the truth shall make you free" (John 8:32). His love frees us from the gnawing pain of inferiority and worthlessness.

While reading this booklet you may have gotten in touch with some very difficult emotions and memories. If so, please remember that neither this book, nor any book, can adequately help you deal with such deep pain. God has made provision for you, though, through an intimate relationship with Him and a renewed connectedness to His body of believers who understand your pain and can guide you through it.

Resolving shame means education, counseling, and/or support groups for all who seek recovery. Some will need intensive treatment. Recovery takes an unknown and extended period of time. It should not be hurried; but one should seek help to prevent the process from being drawn out longer than it has to be.

There are those who can help. Please let them. God wants you to be healthy and whole, full of life and love. May He bless you on your journey.

NOTES

1. Robert S. McGee, Pat Springle, and Jim Craddock, *Your Parents and You* (Houston and Dallas: Rapha Publishing/Word Inc., 1990).

2. Adele Mayer, *Sexual Abuse: Causes, Consequences and Treatment of Incestuous and Pedophilic Acts* (Holmes Beach, CA: Learning Publications, Inc., 1985), p. 6.

3. Robert S. McGee, *The Search for Significance* (Houston: Rapha Publishing, 1990).

4. McGee, *The Search for Significance*.

5. McGee, *The Search for Significance*.

6. Dr. Dan B. Allender, *The Wounded Heart: Hope for Adult Victims of Childhood Sexual Abuse*, with a foreword by Dr. Larry Crabb (Colorado Springs, CO: NavPress, 1990), p. 223.

ABOUT THE AUTHOR . . .

Russ Rainey, Ed.D., received his Doctorate in Psychology and Counseling from Southwestern Baptist Theological Seminary in Ft. Worth. Russ is also a Licensed Professional Counselor and a Certified Alcohol and Drug Abuse Counselor. He served as a counselor for his home church, Fielder Road Baptist, in Arlington, Texas before joining Rapha as Director of Outpatient Services. He is currently the Regional Coordinator of Rapha's *Right Step Training* (a Christian recovery program that focuses on developing support groups within churches). Russ lives in Arlington with his wife, Janet, and his two sons.